PACIFIC

Scott R. Welvaert

Skywater Publishing Cooperative
Chaska, Minnesota

for my girls
Jen, Julia, and Christa

Skywater Publishing Cooperative
Chaska, Minnesota
skywaterpub.com

Library of Congress Cataloging-in-Publication Data
Welvaert, Scott R., 1973—
Pacific / by Scott R. Welvaert.
p. cm. — (Skywater Legacy Poetry Series)
    ISBN 979-8-8692-9751-8 (Ingram pbk)
    ISBN 978-1-938237-98-0 (Amazon pbk)
    ISBN 978-0-9793081-0-9 (pbk. : alk. paper)
    ISBN 978-0-9793081-3-0 (e-book : alk. paper)
I. Title.
PS3623.E5P33 2009
811'.6—dc22   2007028504

Credits
Blake Hoena, editorial direction
Jen Welvaert, cover design
Flat Sole Studio, book layout

Photo Credits
Jennifer Welvaert, author photo
Shutterstock, all (except for author photo)

Acknowledgements
The author and publisher wish to express their grateful appreciation to the following publications in which earlier versions of these poems first appeared: "Index: A Road Trip for Two", *Birmingham Poetry Review*; "Rescue Mission Over Cannon Beach, Oregon", *Cold Mountain Review*; "Marti's Trailer House Living Room", *Jabberwock Review*; "Hospital: Salem, Oregon", *Mankato Poetry Review*; "Losing Her Son to the Ocean" and "What Death Is for David Campbell", *Red Owl Magazine*; "David's Mother", *Rosebud*; "Like a Raccoon", *Roux*; "Piano" and "Painted Rocks in Idaho", *Spire Press*; "A Dodge Charger at Cannon Beach" and "The Last Things", *The Blue Skunk Companion*; "Waiting for Harrison Ford at the End of His Driveway", *Timber Creek Review*; "An Abandoned Church Outside of Ten Sleep" and "Where Wyoming Roads Go", *White Pelican Review*.

INDEX: A ROAD TRIP FOR TWO

MINNESOTA

BUILDING AN AIDS CLINIC

When the masons laid
the floor to this lobby,
did they stop to weigh
each tile in hand, slide

their thumbs down the
smooth side, take pride
in the mortar frame,
moist along all its edges,

or did they shake sad
heads with each advancing
flat stone, the aches dripping
down their backbones,

the pain a sliver to those
who will call this place home?
When the doors open
and this floor is a year old,

those that are dead will still
ride in the patients' eyes,
tracking their black footprints
over drained legs and bones,

and a man will carry a woman
to her car. Together their roads
hang between them, scoop out
the warm mush of their bellies

and if they tipped their bodies
to pour out their AIDS, dry
lakebeds would drink again,
canyon valleys would crack

smiles, and the empty bowls
in the ocean would fill to the brim.

ON FRIDAY NIGHTS

the blues huddle
in the corner of her eye,
push along crows feet
and creeks of mascara.
She backstrokes her
whiskey, its rocks cool
and cumbersome.
She has tried to forget
the blues, to twist her body
like a wet towel and watch
the smoky crooner slide
down the rag of her body, lick
the sweat tumbling down
her breasts, his harmonica lips
warbling her mouth,
cigar smoke blooming
above the bed.

Her whiskey has traveled
the rounds of her stomach
and she tongues the ice
like it's a husband, a lover
who exists between
greasy guitar licks and fingers.
On the way home, the street
is cold, the sidewalk
has a frosty beard, her breath
snows from her mouth. It's here
on this asphalt stage, she slumps
off her clothes, leaves her shell
by the curb, and walks home
under paladin moon.

MARTI'S TRAILER HOUSE LIVING ROOM

Through the window,
her mother loves a man on the couch,
their flanks red like hams,
prime roasts bound in twine.
They are seals barking and slapping each other.
Her fingers press cool against the window,
the wheels in her feet wobble and twist.

She falls asleep on the front step,
listens to the words waving
from the long weeds beside the house,
how the wind bends them with its hands.

In between sleep and waking
she thinks of love as animal,
lions mounting each other in midday sun,
hiding in prowl grass with cubs,
ripping open zebras.

She sees this in herself
as a part of waking each morning,
putting on shoes,
fixing eggs before going to school.

IF AN URN OF ASHES WAS ALLOWED A FEW MORE WORDS

I never had a beer with my son.
But if we had, it would have been a Guinness
with a cream top like sea foam
and a brown cascade of sediment
rolling to lake muck at the glass bottom.
The bar would be cool and dark
with just me, my son and a game of nine-ball.
We would talk about mothers and aprons,
casseroles and kitten oven mitts.

Afterwards we would walk home
under streetlights,
count them out like stars.

I'd tell him how I'd take care of him,
and if it came to the end and his skin
wrapped his bones like butcher paper,
I'd talk about that nine-pound walleye
he caught by Spirit Island,
how life was better with a fish on the line,
how we'd dump our ashes on those island rocks,
let the lake waves lap us away,
scatter those flakes of us,
like a storm cloud beneath lake water.

DAVID'S MOTHER

She settled life
in the layers of her freezer,
lost pieces of wedding cake
wandering between bacon
and a bag of sweet corn.
Three epochs down
is a pair of white baby booties
flat in places where they should
be warm and round.
A carnation smothered
in Saran Wrap sleeps there,
its pink face and leaf-arms
raised against the stem.
Had she known so much beauty
existed with her perishables,
she'd visit the freezer more,
pick up this flower
and hold it cold to the back
of her hand, close her eyes
to see her husband's coffin
and the buttery elation on his face.

Atop the frozen heap,
next to a beef pot pie,
is a shoebox of pictures:
her son behind a bar piano,
his girlfriend like a scarecrow
in white clothes lying on a bed,
him running,
her eating a Twinkie,
both lying on the hood of a car.
In every picture they smile
like licorice and cracks in dry mud,
thin smiles like piano wire
and crescent moons. Now,

when she opens that freezer,
she feels those cold clouds
roll down her legs,
and she can't eat for days.

THE TIRE SWING

She drove sixty miles to sit down with her mom,
but she can't bring herself to step
out of the car, walk past the lawn mower,
stalled with rusty wounds. The grass
cheers victory around it.

Her life tied its slipknot
on top of the tire swing in the front lawn,
her yellow sundress rubbed black,
her thighs red from holding
the rope between her legs, almost a tickle
from a boyfriend's hand.

Had she known her choices would mold
her life into a bracelet of men
each one interchangeable, charming, and plastic,
she would have cut that thick rope
and dragged that old tire to the road.
From the hill she would watch her future
spray the pavement with collected rain,
painting a wet line as it rolls away,
wobbles dead in the grass.

OZONE

Today the rain left its cool, wet breath in the streets
and stepping through it in shorts and bare feet
reminds her of opening a window in winter.
This merging of seasons arouses her,
catches her breathless in her morning walks.
The boulevard ash trees fluff green
after the rain, a green so natural, so alive
that it looks fake.
Her car is the same.
Its hail damage a pale red shimmer under the sun,
but after a storm tumbles through town
the finish looks freshly painted.
The rain has given the neighbors
new cars, driveways, and siding.
Everything has shed its old skin and shines.
She'll walk past all their houses
admiring the clean sidewalks
and the ozone smell that reminds
us there is a higher, more powerful
house cleaner looking after us. A man
will open his front door to pick
up his paper. He will smell that the cleaner
has come and she will think to herself how
the earth finds a way
to rub away its grime and evil.
She'll wave to this man as she passes,
maybe tell him he has a fine square hedgerow.
At the end of block, she turns and runs back.
Her body does what the earth
just did. Rain. The balls of her feet throb
and each breath bleeds down her throat, salty.
Through her front door and into the kitchen,
she pours a cold glass of water, glugs it down.
So cold, it stings. But she feels her body
fluff, her breath cool, her arms and legs weak,
and she feels a little greener on the outside.

WHAT MADE HIM

His favorite time used to be fall,
when the trees tossed down their dry
and crackling mittens
like children home from school.
Each year his street grew deep
with the swash and scrape from people
walking through leaves,
their destinations always two steps ahead.

Half through the raking, his eyebrows
flush with sweat, the groove between
his thumb and finger blistered,
David stopped, leaned against a tree
and closed his eyes to the death in each rustle,
the chaos in each miniature whirlwind of leaves.

The rustle came back with the heroin,
the pinch in the pit of his elbow.
In moments, his whole world grew swollen.
He slogged through each day, smiling.
David the human waterbed. His mother's voice
a blackbird's warble. His father's death a bedtime story.
His body salted to jerky
and his lips bled like broken toilets.

When winter hit, the trees stood like fish bones
over the street, he felt the rustle within him,
weaving its way around his bones, through his veins,
building a nice nest in the trenches between his ribs.

GROUP THERAPY

Outside the clinic, summer hangs the night
like wet laundry. Marti holds a cigarette
with paper fingers, her hands
and shoulders rustle, a leaf pile slowly
eroding in the wind.

Answers stand inside like windmills.
Coping is stirred into cheap coffee,
glazed over complimentary pastries.
It's hard to boil her life down
to a textbook and weekly meetings.

She'll take the black hand
the smoke offers her, suck it down
until her lungs are tight and painful,
a last gasp of air.

Inside David wrings his hands,
a madman, his knuckles bobbing
like whitecaps on his skin.

He sees the zombies
around the circle, the half-eaten meat
to their cheeks and hands, their eyelids
thin and dark.

His future keeps the car running outside.
It's laying on the horn good and hard,
revs the engine with a heavy foot.
Sweat slumps down
his neck. He's noisy when
he leaves. His chair shudders
across the tile floor. The door
chuffs shut with a click.

Outside her smoke gloves his hand,
strings him along to her car,
the engine running.

POSTCARD OF CANNON BEACH

The card grew old with her. Its yellow face
a migrant worker's, wrinkled
from high sun and dusty breeze.
It ripped once and wears its Scotch-tape
battle scar down the middle.
The corners are worn to the nubs, paper frayed
soft and round. It has not lived a day
without her, palmed in a sweaty hand,
a shirt pocket, a lunchbox.
As much as she would like to believe,
it is not her father, just an old photo of the ocean.

Years later the postcard
is still folded in her jeans, her father's words
softer and harder to read
but her eyes are drawn to those rocks,
the low crashing surf. She runs
fingertips over the picture, imagines
a fishing trawler bobbing over waves,
the ocean swatting her father away.

Her father waits for her
between the hunched rocks on the shore.
She too is dead,
her veins drying up,
crumbling like a burnt vine.
This is why she slides
the postcard across the table,
asks her lover to read the words, see the waves
ripple over paper wrinkles, and promise
to slough her body into the surf.

SOUTH DAKOTA

IN THE PASSENGER SEAT

While she sleeps, her lips part
and breath slips between teeth
and tongue. If he were made
of air, her breath would hold

him asleep in her lungs until
he entered her blood stream
and whisked away to her brain.
Its fifty miles before he knows

they're out of Minnesota, leaving
the place where lakes weigh more
than people, where a blond girl
punched her in the nose years ago,

made that space between tip
and eyebrow wider. He wonders
what she looks like with no clothes,
if her skin feels like a spilled milkshake

or if freckles hang over her shoulders,
bundles of small grapes. Maybe
her ribs show like fence pickets
when she stretches upward.

So he grips the wheel with white knuckles,
speeds, watches green road signs blend into one
clean line and the road rises with them,
bends with each of their curves.

DINNER AT THE CORN PALACE CAFE

They pile their plates high with ears of corn,
chitter and whittle each thick yellow stick to the bones —
the hulls fleshy between their teeth.
After each cob is stacked on the table like cord wood —
rotten and chewed — they lift their shirts
and lean back,
display their stomachs like those freckled corn walls,
the bulbs onioned atop the towers
across the street. That night they pull the car over,
and vomit on the gravel shoulder.

They sleep in the car like newborn rabbits.
Her ear fevers on his chest,
and dying in the backseat of a car drums
from concept to lilac reality.
In the morning, disease stops strangling her one last time,
stops puckering her neck with fresh cankers,
and banishes itself to the glove box
with a wrinkled map, a red pen, and bus fare, in case of
        emergencies.

BUFFALO

With her head resting,
pressed to his denim

coat, buffalo take steps
behind her eyelids, hang

their heavy shag chins close
to the ground. Their eyes

are foiled chocolates,
rolling smooth to each bent

weed, seeing the fields
striptease for them. It's then

she blinks with bison eyes,
squints with their independence,

their brash analysis of the prairie,
how the eye doesn't need

the body to survive. It just
needs what is out there,

knocking to come in, lifting
those soft pink doors wide

open so color smears into color,
whirls into dust-devils and dirty

picket fences, the tire swing
hanging from frayed rope,

and off, slightly higher
than chicken hawks circle,

space meets earth in a blue
festival, a piñata broken open,
spilling ice cubes in the sky.

A SOUTH DAKOTA HIGHWAY

Past the windshield,
she watches the moon loop

white threads through
rhinestones in the sky,

and though she swivels
her head to each window,

she can't catch them all.
She can't pluck them from

their denim background
and keep them bundled

in her pocket. She can't
cup them in her hands

like broken glass. She knows
this, but still, she slows the car

by Orion, slips her face out
an open window and lets

her telescopes widen, dilate
to hold the whole picture,

the sequins spilling
over each other.

DRIVING INTO RELIANCE, SOUTH DAKOTA

When she left Minnesota,
the trees fish-boned from the hills
but here, her insides acidic and rotting,
she welcomes the float
her stomach feels
each time the car falls and rises.
Here she can forget about responsibility,
take the time
to hold a rusty STOP sign in her hands.

Reliance is full of these relics
fallen flat to the ground,
their shells bubbling and flaking away.
Outside of town, a barn limps to the side,
its back crooked and sore.
The windmill stands, its petals withered
and blown away. The farmhouse is gone,
leaving the foundation
to flap its gums in the dry grass.
It comforts her to know
that two have survived.
She imagines them an old couple
sharing tea and crossword puzzles in the morning.
Where the house once stood,
David stands on the steps
and knocks on the door that is not there.
No one answers.
He turns and shrugs his shoulders.

This is the man
she has trusted for six days, the face
that presses the windshield each night for Orion,
the man who promised to set her body adrift in the Pacific.
When Reliance blinks out of their rear-view mirror,
she scribbles her finger

down the side of his neck
and he pinches with his neck and shoulder,
and there, in that car,
with a rusted STOP sign in the back seat,
she does not feel like a relic anymore.

ON THE BANKS OF BOX ELDER CREEK

A small bridge spans the creek like a playing card.
Its iron palm invites them to cross,
pause in the middle and lean into the rusty rail.
Below them water shakes hands with the banks,
a wet senator, pressing the flesh. For her,
the river is cool, breath over ice cubes
and as the stream breeze gooses the skin behind her knees,
she feels new again, a wooden toy, freshly sanded.
He too feels the creek stripping AIDS away from them,
imagines the disease caked on them
and the river, cold and white, swallows their thirst,
clears their throats.

Up to their knees, their feet plunge the silt,
and they're both breathless.
The creek bed is a womb, vital and soft.
When they are done and rolling down their pant legs,
they look at their shoes, those ground insulators,
and scrape at the riverbank until their hands are clumped with mud
      and a hole
remains.
They bury their shoes,
to hibernate with the turtles and frogs.
They do this to feel the world again,
to step on the jagged rock,
shuffle in yard grass, and if all goes well,
to kick sand on the lip of the Pacific.

PUSHING A DODGE CHARGER INTO A GAS STATION

Their legs puked a mile ago,
and though his calves are fists,

he grinds each foot to the road,
heaves out his sore shoulder,

a buffalo butting ahead in line.
He does this to impress her.

She has not tired, clumped
to the ground like worn, brown

boots. Her leather has not sagged
on the sides, cracked and dried.

He needs to show her that his
muscles still strangle his bones,

that somewhere inside, disease
has not eaten, has not filled its

belly with warm organs. He
does it for the sweat, the work

they wipe from their brow, the cold
sodas they share in the shade.

BUILDING A FIRE AT CRAZY HORSE

All around them, twilight pours
more indigo over the night

and as he cracks dry sticks
over his knee, sets them popping

on the fire, he thinks of the sticks
buried in his arms, his chest, and legs,

the coat hanger for his sagging skin.
He knows where his bones will be

three months from now: dried and laid
asleep on the prairie, slumped down

in the corner of a greasy, gas station,
or beneath the Pacific intertwined

with the knees and knuckles
of her bones. The fire kicks

smoke and ash above them. At night,
it tans their skin back to life.

Shadows drip behind their ears,
hang on cheekbones. No sound

comes when she talks, only
the wind hauling the Dakotas to every

state east, coating cities with dust.
The fire snaps in front of her, drapes

her face in floating embers. She is a war
chant, his dance for rain. This is how he

wants to remember her: hot faces, burning
snow falling upward, dry lips drawing out

no words, a deafness that is like a distant
song barely alive and crawling into his ears.

SOMEWHERE NEAR THE BLACK HILLS

they hear the lurch and
chunk of the Earth slowing to a stop. The great gears
in the planet creak, cogs wheeze, and after each
machination pings into place
they stand there swaying,
the highest car on a Ferris wheel.
Even the grass holds its breath.

As a girl, she fell off her father's roof,
landed square in a thorny
hedge-row, and now, with the world on its tiptoes,
she is afraid to move. The only direction
she feels is up, her insides strung high
by helium balloons, floating up her throat,
knocking on her teeth to get out.

He is already at Earth's edge,
his fingers gripping its grassy rim. Over
the side, the sun sinks
with all the stars, their light like blonde hairs on end.
The sky is bruising. Those clams that are the Black Hills,
scurry away. He grabs
her, takes her to the world's lip, and places
her hands on it, reminds her of her father's
arm: firm, trustworthy, and familiar.

She grips the grassy
edge like a stone that wants to skip the pond,
like a small plane that begs to loop, like the woman
she is now, hands on the wheel,
the horizon tucked safely in her pocket.

WYOMING

IN THE MORNING

when the sun pops and spills over the horizon,
they see bubbles looping from their perch
high on a Coca-Cola billboard.

She hugs her knees and watches
him, how he sticks his chin into light
and grows golden, whittles down to a thin

stick man. This is when she loves him. It eats
her, strikes pain in her palms and cheeks. Together,
they talk about the land, how Wyoming's belly

is wide and open like them, and they wish this state
would never end. It could repeat itself over
and over, and the morning wouldn't go away,

but stay there, suspended in a clear gel
that only they could move through. Swallows
would be caught in mid-flight poses,

wings spread, heads up. Vulnerable. They could drive
to a gas station, steal orange sodas, a handful of licorice,
stand out front by the gas pumps and drink both bottles

then wipe their mouths with the back of their hands.
The sun would be in the same spot they left it
and nothing could kill them, not AIDS, not a car wreck,

not even drowning in the ocean.
But they drive on, leave their empty bottles to catch
a gas station breeze, blowing two notes over the road.

EATING PEANUT BUTTER SANDWICHES NEAR DEVIL'S TOWER

Behind her, the prairie
is aroused. Its one nipple
stands up to yawn between

the grass, and when she
laughs, she becomes a fawn
feeding on high branches,
her neck flashes its midriff.

The sandwiches are choking with peanut butter.

Behind him, the asphalt
rolls over. It tucks the brush
under its head, pulls the warm

sky over to its side, and when
he stares at her, he becomes
a leopard, slinking between jungle
vines, black lips sheathing white teeth.

FLYING A KITE THAT LOOKS LIKE A BAT

The plastic frame fits snug
in her hands. Its thin black cape
ripples against her belly.

He loves the weight on the other end.
That's why he doesn't want her
to thrust its menacing face

to the wind, and watch the clouds
swat it down to the ground, limbs
broken over each other, skin

torn in jagged folds and curves.
He doesn't want the slack
in the line or the erratic tugs

from the kite cutting through
the air. He wants to step backwards
and rearrange their chess pieces

so they smell apple trees unfolding
their branches again, and the hot,
summer asphalt paving their noses.

He'd like to be young with her
and freckled: grass stains
where no grass should be,

two kids running barefoot
over a lumpy yard, earthworm
mounds punching their arches

and the sidewalks elbow into the hedges.
And if she were gone, it would just be
a street, hot under the sun, and even it

would want her, even the breeze
would like to blow in her ear, rustle
her hair until she laughed like a sprinkler.

TWO PEOPLE STRANDED

With the car dead, the sky taps
wet on the windshield,
headlights pull in the white
lines and a road sign
where a black deer leaps
from a yellow world.

For whatever reason
they run with open mouths.
They let shirtsleeves flap
to the wind, the rain riddle
their hair, hands, and face.
In this field of black grass,
he wants her to form those words
with his mouth, and lie down,
let gravity press through them.

The barn door moans open
and the dry air lifts their noses,
powders them with the musk
and hay of horses. This is when
she undresses, when the slats
and boards let him see
that pink ribbon of her unravel.
She even smiles when turned away,
remembers the sweat on his hands,
the soft yank of his arms,
the guidance through rain.

WAKING UP IN A BARN

Her lungs fill up
like burlap sacks
and her insides
bristle, crack out
and sneeze.

She watches him
sleep in the next stall,
where the window
rains yellow morning.
Each time he breathes,
the dust loops its ribbon
arms, and the barn
heaves its dry chest.

Romance is the itch
dripping down her
arms, the prick of each
tick bite, the feathery
cadence of spider legs
across her ankles.

She rakes each groove
and welt red, until her
skin is a jagged network,
a connect-the-dots
finished, pink, and swollen.

WASHING IN CRAZY WOMAN CREEK

In the river, she rubs
off the grease that has
frosted her body,
caked her scalp with
the sun overhead,
and when she lifts

her arms and forms
an H with that river
water, he imagines
she is peeling away
her diseased skin.
With each thin flake,

her whiteness floats
away, and the woman
standing before him
flushes pink and full,
eyelashes thick like
mossy tree branches,

cheeks held up by
piano wire in her
smile. For him, it's
hard to think that
death ran its hands
through her hair,
painted its nasty

red face over her
back and neck,
pocked each swollen
sore from ankle to
collarbone. He knows
the river is the place

to leave your dead things,
so he carries her sleeping
to the car, and revs
the engine west.

WAITING TO MEET HARRISON FORD AT THE END OF HIS DRIVEWAY

If they stand on their tiptoes and weave their heads
around the gate and trees, they can see him hammering
a rail to a fence, his shirt wet in the armpits,
a tool belt hanging off one hip. From a distance
he is any man in any town, fixing a fence, sweating
his shirt.

In her mind, he is her father raising his hand
to a troublesome daughter, a girl who bends
the nails while hammering and bangs crescent moons
into the wood, and as his father,
he is saving a life, his arm stretched past the roof's edge,
taut and sinewy, catching a fallen son
who chased a shingling nail too far.

They split a sack lunch and sit
down outside his gate and lean back to the midday sun.
They close their eyes and his pounding
rifles through the valley like a bullwhip, like a starship
jumping into lightspeed.

When they awake, their cheeks
are burned and tight, tanned like a horse's saddle,
and the sandwiches are gone.
There is a note in its place:
You make a damn fine sandwich, young lady.
His hammering dances between the trees all around them.

AN ABANDONED CHURCH OUTSIDE TEN SLEEP

They stop for the irony,
to fall asleep ten feet out of Ten Sleep
and when their headlights cool,
the sky yawns wide and black.
Stars glisten like shiny caps, bright fillings
packed in places the universe missed.

They climb to the back seat
where they harbor close like puzzle pieces,
children napping in red wagons,
and the pillow that is Wyoming
catches their tired faces in its hands.

The morning sets a church next to the road.
Crippled, it hunkers down on its knees,
step-boards warped,
paint molting to the ground like snow.
Above them, the bell has rusted away
the last of its rings. It creaks in the wind,
the lisp after a stroke.

They eat their lunch inside this church,
sitting cross-legged on the floor. The stained glass
window glows for them in the morning sun,
reminds them of a robin under a bush,
shaking the rain from its feathers.

WHERE WYOMING ROADS GO

Seeing this land
makes him glad that she is driving.
He does not have to stare
at this plain, white, tee-shirt of America,
but at this woman,
driving.

One hand out the window,
thumping the roof to some song,
Touch Me,
she makes steering look like smoking.
She lounges back,
her left leg bent at the knee,
drawn up on the seat,
smoke rings even wisp off the wheel.

He couldn't care less where this road goes
as long as this woman
fills the space next to his.
He dips his remaining days in her face —
mushroom under-belly eyes, hair
snaking in the breeze
like Wyoming roads, and lips
that part the earth and sky when she sees him.

IDAHO

SPYING ON HER SWIM

Over the water, ripples
cast out their medallions,

wave their peso faces
along the shore. The dock

wants to release its tired
boards, slide its nails

to the weeds, a wet burial.
Wrapped in her own nutshell,

she quivers at the edge.
The water between her toes

offers itself, murmurs a note
on wet paper and when she

spreads herself to the sun,
opens her china cabinet doors,

the cups beneath her shirt push
out their elegance, soften
her porcelain edges.

WASHING HANDS IN A GAS STATION BATHROOM

She wonders if he could ever love
the reflection in this smudged mirror.

If he were a cowboy she knows he'd
step in front of a drawn gun, tip his hat

to her, even go to church with an unshaven
face and clay dust on his black boots.

After the villain rode away,
the sun would hide behind his head
and he'd say, "Howdy, ma'am."

She wishes she had a box of Band-Aids
so she could smooth each one over

her sores, cover her hips and elbows
until she became a patchwork,

a shell of flesh strips over white skin,
leaving only slivers for him to see.

PLAYING FOOTBALL

When the ball falls past
and she chases through grass,
she looks younger.

Her body shrinks and clothes
hang limp around her knees
and shoulders, her face

smoothed soft around the edges.
There is blackness in her eyes
and even though she smiles,

he feels helpless, a tree leaning
years into a river.
After it is old and leafless,

it buries itself in the water
until its last finger dips under.
He throws the ball hoping it

will break some mirror in the sky,
that somehow time will shatter
into tiny blue crystals, but it doesn't.

Her nose bleeds, dribbles over her cheeks
and tee shirt and this is her beauty,
the hurt waxing in the corners

of her eyes, hands held in fists,
fingernails digging into palms.
The dark spot on her shirt grows,

each drip sticks wet on her chest,
and he lets her blood fill the cracks
in his lips like salt water one state away.

PIANO

To him, the keys
are pale fingers,
the flats are greased
nails of a mechanic.
With each stiff note
the clank and clatter
of auto repair comes
back: the slick coat
of a crescent wrench
slipping out of grip,
the incessant click
of a ratchet coughing
up rusty bolts.

It's quieting in the way
small waterfalls are quiet
or when the world falls
mute with the windows
rolled up and he can hear
her eyes roll at their base,
the sudden clap of each lid,
the slow wash of lashes.

Somewhere in that piano
he knows a combination
of notes, a special code
that tumbles her to a place
where safety is a running
engine, where they drive
away from sidewalks
and boulevard pines
knowing the sun sleeps
heavily over the side
of the road, where love

is in the arc of a wiper blade,
in her hand clearing
windshield fog.

PAINTED ROCKS IN IDAHO

She leaves him in the shower, borrows
the car but doesn't bother with clothes.
The leather cracks in the seat
slice their signature on her hips and back.

The popcorn rattle of rain on the hood
offers no advice-
no wisdom, no singing telegram.
She looks for things that tell her to go back to him:
a doe raising her head from the forage,
a crow lifting off a stop sign,
the muskrat broken and spread over the road.

Around her, Norway Pines wipe
cheap mascara from the sky
and the fat rain slathers itself heavy
with thick lacquer over the brush and grass.

Car parked, she steps out
into a downpour, the gravel slick under her feet.
In front of her, rocks jut from the mist and snarl
their Krylon faces. This is the sign, she thinks.
The painted rock she
rolls in her hands is a ladybug,
the sunflower sketched on granite bends
with an imaginary wind.

In the rear-view mirror, she sees a Chinese dragon sulking
in the mists behind her, stone after
boulder after rock,
pointing the way home.

AT MIDNIGHT

On the steps to the Border
Motel she knows it's time
to go. The squeaks from

the log walls tug at her
shoulders, brush the cold
off her neck and nose.

The red oaks and pines
step aside for her, raise
their wrinkled heads

and each root, each stone
claws her feet, sketches
footprints into her, red

and jagged. She limps
back on shreds, thanks
the ground for the fight,

for the bloody markers
left on the forest floor.
When she pours between

the bed sheets and holds
his ribcage like a melon,
she weighs his skin,

the gentle lift and settle
of each breath.

LIKE A RACCOON

Outside his motel room,
the rain writes his name
on the ground. The leaves

chatter, excited to be moist
and alive again. He sees
the leaf in him, wishes his

liquids were not retreating.
Each night, before he sleeps,
his blood rolls back and his

veins go flat like cheap straws.
He never knows where his
body fluids go to get away

from him, he can only hear
the shuffle from the rain's
random dance. A raccoon

huddles under a tree, its coat
wet and fluffed. Cleaning,
its claws rove like a Zamboni.

When it finishes, the animal
lumbers home to its rabid wife,
its pestilent children. He watches

until it is quiet again, until his
breath is a ghost on cold glass.

A NIGHT IN IDAHO WOODS

In a forest of spruce and pine,
she finds one willow tree,
uprooted, tipped on its side

during a windstorm. Its dirty
roots yawn from trunk
to ground. Under its great beam,

she sleeps. The afternoon, drunk
in its humidity, bogs down in haze
and scatters the sunlight from

tree to tree. This warmth feels safe
to her, and it's here, beneath
this willow chandelier, this lamp shade

golden for a short time, that she leaves
her eyes shut, turns off her mind,
and lets moss press its hands to her feet.

The sky squints before closing its eyes
and he guides himself tree to tree
with the moon, widowed and bitter. By

morning, his throat is tender and bleeds
for her, but he only hears her name,
an echo, skirting along beaver

ponds and ravines. If he could, he'd raise
the windrow over his shoulders and look
under its rug, but his muscles shake

like gelatin, and acorns bite each foot.
When he finds her, they can rest, lie in bed
like vegetables, huddle close in their carrot

arms, their ripe breasts. Back at the motel, when
he peels off shirt and pants, he finds her asleep,
fresh in the sheets, her skin sun-ripened to his hands.

CATCHING AN OLD COUPLE SHOWERING IN A THUNDERSTORM

The lightning lights their way
along a gravel path
to a harbor of pup tents flickering,
Chinese lanterns hobbling
in the wind. Between thunder,
rain pitters at them, drowns them like house cats.
He shivers, cups his hands around his breath
and she is thinner when wet,
her tee-shirt clingy and aroused.

Ahead, in the black grass,
singing bobs on the storm,
a toy boat loose in a savage wind.

and I
can't
help
falling in love
with
you.

Stepping closer
they see an old couple.
Someone's grandparents,
naked and frothing.
They lather each other's backs,
under their wattling arms
and as quickly as the suds cake their skin
the rain wipes it away,
exposes their drooping breasts,
their dormant genitalia.
They touch each other like curious children,
and run until they fall down, grappling each other.

OREGON

A LAST BIRTHDAY

This is the year
she grows older than her older sister,
the same year
she will leave everything she knows
on the ocean floor.
Blowing out the candles
doesn't come easy.
It picks apart her breath
to imagine her sister
forever twenty-five.

Heaven is a boring place for the young,
they have so little to talk about,
to be proud of.
They wander about
pretending to know how war
is a sharp blow to the temple,
how motherhood
can drain your blood. Her sister
never knew these things,
and neither did she,
but she tried.

She whitewashed herself
in what this globe had to offer.
This is why she can think of Death
as comic relief. She knows
that it rides in her sidecar
hand drawing the map as they go,
a small cotter pin away from separation.

ROADS

Loose gravel shucks from tires when
cars swerve from road to shoulder, their

cursive loops arc behind them in black
rubber streaks. This highway whores

with each red and chrome convertible,
the rust-pocked Charger and Harley.

Each tire roams over the road, massaging
heat buckles in the asphalt, the curves

and dips, hitting those rain-filled potholes,
the rumble strip that vibrates each car

to tell them where to go. Like an oak head-
board, the highway tallies its pleasure

at the roadside Yield. Merge. Bump. Detour.
Reduce Speed. Rest Stop. The highway does

not worry about the mudslides that eat it
away in spring, the construction needed to patch up

its one-night lifestyle. To the road only drifters
matter. The cars with their Firestone hands

come and go, and old highways die, easily
replaced by youthful, more attractive roads.

HOSPITAL: SALEM, OREGON

He knows her eyes can open,
but she sleeps, allows the tubes
to grasp for lungs, clog her chest
with pharmaceutical plastic.
Electronic lizards watch over, lick
her arms, stick tongues into her
veins, let saliva drip into her, curing
her, and he wants to forget she's sick,
a thin clamshell lying there, insides
washed out with the foaming surf.

She wishes they never left Minnesota.
The winter drank them like hot
apple cider, where they washed each
lesion, with Epsom salt and a warm rag,
and they stayed awake at night helping
each other to the bathroom to vomit,
to empty their bellies until they cried
to be carried back to bed, back to sleep.

But they're here, in a hospital, two hours
from the ocean, two time zones from
home, and she knows it was meant to
end better, that the wind was supposed
to knock them over, weaken their knees
like kites, and they would fall into the tide,
let the foam fill their hair and clothes, let
the sand find those folds where arms
and legs meet, that feeling of the grit in
their ears, and with every hand the water
gives them, they slide farther out.

WHAT DEATH IS FOR MARTI REED

In her hospital room,
tubes blossom from her veins.
These things throw a warmth on her,
a sterile, suffocating breeze
that makes her feel like a withered tree,
a willow, bare and dry
bending its neck to the tree cutter's saw.

In the world's grand circuitry
she has sparked her course.
Her last hours will be recorded in this pale room,
where a browning fern waits with
a painting of a tiger on the wall
and the bible
safe and secure in the top drawer of her end table.

She would rather close her eyes,
imagine him awake
next to her
as he yanks out the tubes like tiny snakebites,
lifts her in his arms,
and carries her away.

But when she opens her eyes
it is not like that.
The room heaves its last breath
and he is still asleep next to her,
and the death in these walls is only hers.

SPEEDING AWAY FROM A HOSPITAL

The windows are down. Autumn
puffs the dust off the dashboard,

lifts their hair in clumps. Sweat
gels on their necks. He is desperate.

She is dying. Rubber hoses reach
out of her in a tangle, a litter of dead,

hollow snakes. The plastic bag, drunk
on the floor, swaggers above the engine's

hum. Medicine drools out and over her
feet. The steering wheel sticks to his

skin. He remembers a spilled milkshake.
Vanilla and cold like her hands. Cold, like her

hands. The road waves beneath them,
an asphalt waterbed, warm and soothing.

He holds his breath and the car slows.
Everything around him caramelizes.

He thinks this saves her. As long as
stillness remains, she will not die. But

his lungs spark like a spot welder,
into salty, pink breath, and the world
is racing again: the car, his veins, her.

A DODGE CHARGER AT CANNON BEACH

doors left open
keys dangle like forks in the ignition
a Polaroid of a man playing a piano
rosary beads hang from the rear view mirror
a wet handprint on the dashboard
chip in the windshield looks like a cat's eye
an open black leather purse with a silver clasp
a paper bag filled with beef jerky wrappers
tissues with spots of dried blood
a Polaroid of a woman in white pajamas
three tan bottles of prescription pills
two unrolled sleeping bags tossed in the back seat
one condom, foil folded at the corners
driver's side empty
passenger empty
I.V. tubes strewn about
on the floor a plastic bag of saline bleeds
a hospital bracelet on the ground outside the driver's door
the dome light flickers
one set of footprints heading toward the water

DEATH FOR DAVID CAMPBELL

The day he died,
the sun stared him down through cheesecloth
spread over the sky,
and drug him, heavy and wet from the ocean,
his heels licking up the Oregon sand,
his furrows weaving through pine forests,
the Rockies,
cutting dry riverbeds through the Badlands,
through the chalk
that people call Minnesota winter air,
and once there
the sun dumped him,
sloughed him like a lifetime of dead skin,
and resumed its telltale perch in the sky.

He met a woman who would take him away
from the only soil he smelled,
sod that stuck to his high school football helmet,
the gravel he kicked at
when the disease set in.
He left with her and found his remaining days
inside beef jerky and Twinkies,
in her feverish face as she slept,
her skin spitting like his,
the motel room sticky with pine,
their love sappy and pungent on their underwear.

When he carried her out of the hospital
strangled dry
and skinny in rubber hoses,
she slept on his shoulder
and he gave every cell,
every synapse,
until they wore the ocean cold and wet,
a mitten thrown to the floor,
after shoveling snow.

THE LAST THING

that clawed past
her eyes
wasn't his jaw,
gritty and wet,
pressing to her lips
or the ocean
with its hungry
current below.
It wasn't this water
that wore
them like love,
fed their words
to those gulls,
to the ocean perch
hungry to surface.
It wasn't those days
they carried
in their hands
like a plastic green
basket, the nights
they spent driving,
or the storms,
soaking their chins
with fat splashes,
cutting rivers behind
their ears and down
their necks.

It was a wave
like white ice.
Somewhere far
behind it,
a Minnesota street
lies down,
its sides plump

and frosted.
The trees scratch
upward, past the gray,
toward a season that
took away their leaves.
Down that street
a plow flashes
its blue eyes,
the metal blade
scrapes slow
and closer, until
the snow curls
over the curb,
over her.

OVER CANNON BEACH

Like a patch of cattails, watchers sway
near the shore. Some wish for resolution,
for the crackle of a radio,
a rope ladder to fall
from the sky, dip
its last rung in the water.
They'll hold their breath until
wet hands break
the surface.
Choppers weave between
giant rocks hunched in the shallows,
shining their spotlights like cat-eyes.

No one knows this:
clinging to the rocks, he holds
her body like a bag of wet leaves.
Her hair fans out in the water,
a thin green weed,
and he thinks of how the Wyoming
sunset fed on his arms
and bronzed her face when she laughed,
her eyes doped in the hospital,
how the shivers crept up his legs
as he walked her in, eyelashes wet and heavy,
the water pulling the breath from his lungs.

LOSING HER SON TO THE OCEAN

She stands on the lip
of a cliff, watches
the ocean belt out
its nausea, and sees
two white flecks
on the waves.

The water crumples
grey to the world
but for her it
slices bright and blue,
cups her son and his lover
in wet fingers.

She wants to bellow, to jump in
and hook their arms
to hers, but she dwindles,
and down the swells, waves
raise their crooked smiles
again and again.

ABOUT SCOTT R. WELVAERT

Scott lives in Minnesota with his wife, two daughters, and a deaf husky named Rocket. He has authored numerous books, including *The Curse of the Wendigo*, *The Mosquito King*, *The Alabaster Ring*, *Grotesque*, and *The 13th Floor*. An avid outdoorsman and comic book nerd, he enjoys writing stories that bend the fabric of reality and offer something more than this world can conjure.

OTHER POETRY TITLES BY SKYWATER

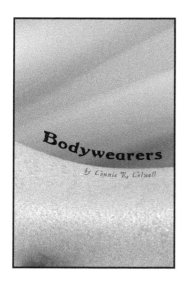

Bodywearers
Connie R. Colwell
Whether Miller writes of a red-tailed hawk hunting for mice or a lover's underwear crumpled up on the bedroom floor, her voice is filled with a revealing breath of candor, drawing our attention to the small details in nature and of the body, often showing us beauty where we may not have expected it.

Gigs
John Davis
Blues in D minor, big bellies over factory belts, and Elvis Presley license plates-Gigs is a collection of poems that shows us the gentle beauty of ordinary life. Davis's language breathes, without labor. His metaphors fit tight. And the rhythm of each word keeps pace with our innermost beats. Absolutely every poem in this book hammers a rightly strung cord.

To learn more about
Skywater Publishing Cooperative
and our upcoming releases,
visit us at *https://skywaterpub.com*
or scan the QR code below

Milton Keynes UK
Ingram Content Group UK Ltd.
UKHW010817220424
441551UK00002B/294

9 798869 297518